KOALA

by Caroline Arnold
Photographs by
Richard Hewett

Mulberry Books
New York

PHOTO CREDITS: Permission to use the following photographs is gratefully acknowledged: Roy Hunter, pp. 15, 16, 17.

Library of Congress Cataloging-in-Publication Data: Arnold, Caroline. Koala. Summary: Describes the habitat, varieties, physical characteristics, feeding habits, and other behavior of this marsupial, focusing on one individual animal and her baby in an Australian sanctuary. 1. Koalas—Juvenile literature. [1. Koalas] I. Hewett, Richard, ill. II. Title.
QL737.M39A76   1987   599.2   86-18092   ISBN 0-688-11503-9

Acknowledgments

Many people have helped us on this project. We thank Qantas Airways and Terry Bransdon of the Australian Information Service, whose generous assistance made it possible for us to go to Australia to research and photograph the book. We thank the staff of Lone Pine Koala Sanctuary in Brisbane, Australia, and Pat Robertson (pictured above), owner and director, who so graciously gave us their time and cooperation. In particular we thank Peter Douglas, Terry Carmichael, Paul O'Callaghan, Mark Brumm, and Roy Hunter. We are also grateful to Tony Wood, Bryan Nothling, Don Burnett of the Eprapah Environmental Center, Neville and Jane Davis, and John Hughes for their assistance. Lastly, we want to thank our editor, Andrea Curley, for her enthusiasm and encouragement throughout this project.

Moving nimbly among the branches, Frangipani found a new resting place. Then, extending her long, furry arm, she reached out for a new leaf. As she ate it, she could hear the other koalas that lived at the Lone Pine Koala Sanctuary in Brisbane, Australia, moving about on nearby branches. Like most of the koalas at the sanctuary, Frangipani had been born there. She had been named after a tropical flower that grows in Australia. Now Frangipani was three years old. One month earlier she had mated with one of the male koalas. Soon she would be having her own baby.

During the early years of Australia's settlement by the English, koalas filled the forests along the eastern and southeastern coasts. However, their numbers began to grow smaller as many of them were killed for their soft fur. Later, as cities expanded and forests were chopped down to make room for houses, people began to fear that the koala would disappear altogether and become extinct. Laws were passed to protect koalas, and special parks and preserves were established so people could see koalas up close and learn more about them. The parks also provided a safe place for the koalas to live.

Today, some of the koalas born at these preserves are put back into the wild in places where koalas once lived but have since disappeared. Others are sent to zoos. People all over the world seem to love these furry creatures that look more like stuffed toys than live animals.

Victoria koala

New South Wales koala

The scientific name for the koala is *Phascolarctos cinereus,* which, in Latin, means furry, pouched, gray bear. Although the koala looks like a toy teddy bear, it is not a bear at all. It is more closely related to animals like opossums.

There are three varieties of koalas. The largest, the Victoria koala, lives in southern Australia. Its darker color and shaggy fur help to keep it warm in cold weather. The New South Wales koala is middle-sized and has shaggier ears than the smaller Queensland koala. Frangipani and the other koalas at the Lone Pine Sanctuary are the Queensland type.

Queensland koala

Male koalas are larger and more muscular than females. A mature male Queensland koala can weigh up to 17½ pounds (approximately 8 kilograms). A female usually weighs only 12 pounds (about 5.5 kilograms). Koalas reach full size when they are four years old.

Except for mating, males do not normally associate with females. After the female becomes pregnant, she leaves the male and waits alone for her baby to be born. Only one baby is born at a time. Most female koalas breed only once every two years, usually between the months of September and June. Both males and females are ready to breed when they are about three years old.

Most mammals that live in Australia, including the koala, are marsupials. Like other mammals, female marsupials give birth to live young, which they nourish with their milk. However, unlike other mammals, a female marsupial has a special pouch on her underside in which her baby is carried and fed during its early months of life.

Male koala

Female koala

When a marsupial baby is born, it has barely begun to develop and is very small. At birth, a koala baby is only three-fourths of an inch (nineteen millimeters) long.

A koala baby is born after a pregnancy of only five weeks. It is blind, hairless, and about the size of a lima bean. At birth, it uses its strong forelimbs to crawl from the opening of the birth canal, along its mother's belly, and into her pouch. This six-inch journey takes about three minutes. It is a dangerous trip, and if the baby loses its way or gets knocked off, it will not survive.

Once inside the pouch, the baby attaches itself to one of its mother's two teats. The teat swells inside the baby's mouth and holds the tiny koala safely in place. For the next seven to eight months, the baby stays inside the pouch and sucks milk from the teat. Gradually, it grows into a tiny, furry koala.

Few people have ever seen a koala birth. This koala baby fell off and died before it reached its mother's pouch. It was preserved to show how tiny a newborn koala really is.

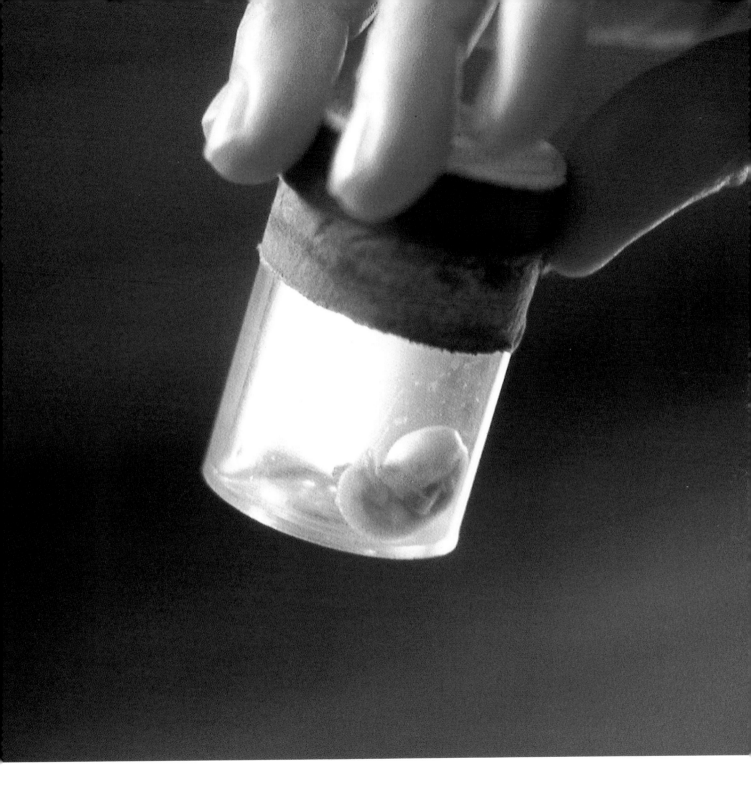

While Frangipani's baby was grow-ing, a strong muscle across the open-ing of the pouch kept it tightly closed. Then, when the baby was ready to come out, the muscle relaxed.

The little koala wiggled around un-

til its head was at the opening of the pouch. Then, pushing until the opening widened, the baby finally took its first peek at the outside world.

For a week after its first appearance, the koala baby did not come all the way out of the pouch but simply peered out from time to time. If it got frightened, it ducked back into the safety of the pouch. When the baby koala wanted to sleep or drink, it stayed inside.

When Frangipani's baby was ready to come all the way out of the pouch for the first time, it reached out to grasp its mother's fur. Slowly it pulled itself onto its mother's belly, and there it clung tightly in the safety of Frangipani's lap. The baby koala was now about eight inches (twenty centimeters) long. It looked just like its mother, but it was much smaller.

A baby koala can be examined only after it comes out of the pouch. When the people at Lone Pine looked at Frangipani's baby and discovered that it was a female, they named her Karen, after a friend of the owner of the preserve.

Frangipani flowers

All of the koalas at Lone Pine are given names. Some, like Karen, are named after people. Others, like Frangipani, are named after flowers. The koalas are also identified by numbers that show when they arrived at the sanctuary. Karen's number, 175, shows that she was the seventeenth koala to arrive in 1985.

By the end of 1985, there were over twenty new koalas at Lone Pine. Of these, four would be chosen to go to the San Francisco Zoo the following year. As long as Karen stayed in good health, it was likely that she would be one of those sent. Each year some of the koalas at Lone Pine go to new homes. Otherwise, Lone Pine Koala Sanctuary would become overly crowded.

When Karen became older she would have her number tattooed on her ear. The procedure is quick and painless and insures that each koala at the koala sanctuary will be properly identified.

During the first four weeks out of the pouch, a young koala goes in and out. But after about a month, it is too big to stay in the pouch any longer. Then it just pops its head inside when it wants a drink of milk.

A young koala normally stays with its mother until it is about eleven months old. During this time it continues to drink her milk. At the same time, it learns to eat leaves. At first, the mother produces pellets of partly digested leaves for her baby to eat. Soon, however, the young koala learns how to find leaves on its own.

An adult koala eats over two pounds (one kilogram) of leaves, buds, and stems each day. A koala has two sharp teeth in the front of its mouth that are good for tearing leaves or stripping bark. In the back of its mouth it has five pairs of flat chewing teeth.

A koala has a large nose and an excellent sense of smell. It sniffs each leaf before eating. If the leaf does not smell right, the koala will try a different one.

The favorite foods of koalas are the leaves of eucalyptus, or gum, trees. They prefer the tender, light green shoots that grow on the tips of the branches. Each species of eucalyptus tree is "in tip" only a few months of the year, with each kind of tree having its own growing season. So koalas in the wild must keep moving from tree to tree to find food.

There are about six hundred different species of eucalyptus trees in Australia, but only between thirty-five and fifty of them are eaten by koalas. In the north, koalas prefer forest red gum, river red gum, tallowwood, swamp mahogany, gray gum, and scribbly gum. In the south, Sydney blue gum, swamp gum, and ribbon gum are favored.

When koalas cannot get their favorite food and are forced to eat other kinds of leaves, they tend to be less healthy and may even die. In areas where forests have been cut down, forest rangers encourage people to replant with the type of trees that koalas like to eat.

Koalas that are kept in zoos or sanctuaries need to have a good supply of suitable leaves nearby. At Lone Pine the koalas are provided with a variety of fresh leaves once a day. Staff members drive up to forty miles to cut leaves for them.

The climate of California is similar to Australia's. It is the only place in the United States where koalas can be kept in zoos. Australia has also sent koalas to zoos in Japan. In both these places, special eucalyptus forests have been planted to provide food for these animals.

A long time ago, the aborigines, or native Australians, thought that the koala was an animal that did not drink, and their name, "koala," means "drinks no water." In fact, koalas do sometimes drink, although the firm, oily eucalyptus leaves provide most of the water they need.

Koalas are nocturnal animals, which means that they are more active at night than during the day. Even so, a koala spends most of its life—day and night—asleep. To sleep, a koala simply wedges its body into the fork of a tree, wraps its arm or leg around a branch for safety, and closes its eyes. It may wake up from time to time, grab a few bites to eat, and then go back to sleep.

When it is rainy or cold, a koala does not have to seek shelter. Its thick fur is waterproof and provides plenty of warmth. During hot weather, it sheds some of its fur.

Like all babies, Karen grew quickly. Every two weeks she and her mother were weighed. By subtracting the weight of the cage and of Frangipani from the total, Karen's weight and growth rate could be determined.

When a young koala first comes out of the pouch, it rides on its mother's underside. As it gets older, it learns to ride "piggyback." By the time Karen had been out of the pouch a month, she had learned to crawl onto her mother's back. Her strong grip held her firmly in place, and she was in no danger of falling off, even as Frangipani climbed.

Even with a young koala on her back, a mother can move about easily. Both the hands and feet of koalas are used to grasp branches, and each hand has an extra thumb that helps to give an even tighter grip.

Koalas are well-adapted to their life in the treetops. Their strong fore-limbs, sharp claws, and good sense of balance make them excellent climbers. At times they even leap, like acrobats, from branch to branch. The only time a koala walks on the ground is in search of a new tree.

Usually koalas are peaceful animals, although their needle-sharp claws and strong teeth can be fearful weapons. Koalas do not attack people or other animals except in defense. Normally, when in danger, a koala prefers to scramble quickly to the top of the tallest tree.

A male koala has a scent gland on his chest that he uses to mark his territory. He does this by rubbing the scent onto branches and leaves. If any other male comes into his territory, he will try to chase it away.

Sometimes male koalas fight with each other during the mating season. Then they push and try to grab each other's ears. At the same time they hoot at each other in a low, hollow growl. After such fights at Lone Pine, the animals' ears are checked for injuries so they can be treated if necessary.

Koalas do not have many natural enemies. Young koalas can be endangered by large birds or snakes, but usually they are protected by their mothers. Wild dogs, called dingoes, will kill a koala if they find one on the ground.

The koala's greatest enemy today is human beings. In the dark it is hard for a driver to see a koala crossing the road. A young koala in the enclosure next to Karen's was orphaned when his mother was killed by a car. Luckily, the younger animal was found by people before he got hurt, too. When he was brought in to Lone Pine, he was just old enough to be able to take care of himself, and he adapted, or adjusted, to his new home quickly. In areas where koalas are known to live, signs warn drivers to watch carefully for any koalas that might be on the road.

As Karen grew older she became less dependent on Frangipani. She was eager to explore the world on her own. Normally, koala babies stay with their mothers until they are about eleven months old. By then they no longer need to drink their mother's milk, and they stop riding piggyback. At that age they weigh about four pounds (two kilograms) and are about one quarter the size of an adult. They are ready to live alone. When Karen was weaned, that is, taken away from her mother, she was put into a different enclosure. After Karen left, Frangipani was ready to mate again.

At Lone Pine the koalas are kept in small groups. Each open-air enclosure has several perches and plenty of food, and the koalas live peacefully together. However, in the wild, where food is harder to find, koalas normally live alone, except during the mating season. Then a male may collect a harem of two or three females.

Soon it was time to choose the koalas that would be sent to the San Francisco Zoo. Four young females would be chosen. All of them had to be completely healthy. One by one, they were examined by the veterinarian. Then blood samples were taken and checked to make sure that none of them were carrying any diseases. One of the biggest problems for koala colonies is infectious disease. A disease that had recently swept through many of the wild colonies caused many deaths, and females that became sick with it could no longer have any babies. Scientists are now trying to develop vaccines that will prevent such diseases from spreading.

Koalas in the wild usually live to be about ten years old. In captivity, with good care, they often live to be twelve or thirteen.

After her examination, Karen was found to be in excellent health. She would be one of the koalas going to San Francisco. While waiting to leave, Karen and the other koalas were kept in a special enclosure. There they would not be exposed to any other koalas that might be sick.

Finally, the day arrived for the long journey. The koalas were placed in special traveling cages. Each cage had several large posts for resting and was filled with fresh eucalyptus leaves. Then the cages were covered and loaded onto a truck so that they could be taken to the airport. There the koalas, in their cages, were put into the cargo compartment of the airplane.

Soon the plane took off. During the long flight, people regularly checked on the animals to make sure they were all right. Even though the airplane noise was loud and a bit frightening, the darkness and familiar leaves in the cages helped make the koalas feel at home. Still, the keepers were glad when the plane landed. Soon, Karen and the other koalas were on their way to the zoo.

The koala house at the San Francisco Zoo was roomy, quiet, and filled with fresh leaves. Karen and the other koalas from Lone Pine quickly got used to their new home. Because they had grown up in captivity, they were used to living closely with other koalas and to having people nearby. At the zoo, just as at Lone Pine, visitors came to take pictures and to learn about koalas.

All over the world the koala is a symbol of Australia. Koalas are a favorite exhibit in zoos and can be seen on television and in advertisements. Yet in the wild, they must often struggle to survive. As people around the world learn more about koalas and become more aware of their needs, the future will become more secure for this gentle ambassador of goodwill.

Index

Dear Parents and Educators,

Welcome to Penguin Young Readers! As parents and educators, you know that each child develops at their own pace—in terms of speech, critical thinking, and, of course, reading. Penguin Young Readers recognizes this fact. As a result, each Penguin Young Readers book is assigned a traditional easy-to-read level (1–4) as well as an F&P Text Level (A–P). Both of these systems will help you choose the right book for your child. Please refer to the back of each book for specific leveling information. Penguin Young Readers features esteemed authors and illustrators, stories about favorite characters, fascinating nonfiction, and more!

Mo Jackson: Get on the Ice, Mo!

LEVEL 3

F&P TEXT LEVEL **J**

This book is perfect for a **Transitional Reader** who:
• can read multisyllable and compound words;
• can read words with prefixes and suffixes;
• is able to identify story elements (beginning, middle, end, plot, setting, characters, problem, solution); and
• can understand different points of view.

Here are some **activities** you can do during and after reading this book:
• Adding -ing to words: One of the rules when adding -ing to words is, when a word ends with an -e, take off the -e and add -ing. With other words, you simply add the -ing ending to the root word. The following words are -ing words in this story. On a separate piece of paper, write down the root word for each word: *helping, facing, skating, letting*. Next, add -ing to the following words from the story: *look, crash, get, put, take, walk, start*.
• Summarize: Work with the child to write a short summary about what happened in the story. What happened in the beginning? What happened in the middle? What happened at the end?

Remember, sharing the love of reading with a child is the best gift you can give!

*This book has been officially leveled by using the F&P Text Level Gradient™ leveling system.

For my joyful grandson, Ari—DAA

For John Kutch, who taught us to skate—SR

PENGUIN YOUNG READERS
An imprint of Penguin Random House LLC, New York

First published in the United States of America by Penguin Young Readers,
an imprint of Penguin Random House LLC, New York, 2022

This paperback edition published by Penguin Young Readers,
an imprint of Penguin Random House LLC, New York, 2023

Visit us online at penguinrandomhouse.com.

Library of Congress Control Number: 2022019029

Manufactured in China

ISBN 9780593352755   10 9 8 7 6 5 4 3 2 1 WKT

GET ON THE ICE, MO!

by David A. Adler
illustrated by Sam Ricks

"Skate to me,"

Mo's dad says.

"Skate to me."

"Wee!" Mo calls out.

He looks at his skates as

he slides across the ice.

CRASH!

"No, no," his dad tells him.

"Don't look down.

Look ahead."

Mo gets up.

He tries again.

CRASH!

He falls again.

"Hi, Mo."

"Hi, Amy.

My dad is helping me get

ready for the game."

"I'll help, too.

I need to practice."

Mo and Amy put on

their helmets.

They take their sticks

and skate.

Amy slides

across the ice.

She even skates

backward.

Mo skates and falls.

He gets up and tries again.

He falls again.

Amy tells him, "You don't look
at your feet when you walk.
Don't look at your feet
when you skate."

Amy drops a puck
on the ice.

She hits it to Mo.

Whoosh!

The puck hits Mo's stick
and bounces off.

It slides toward the net.

"Nice shot!" Amy calls out.

"But I didn't do anything!"

"Yes you did," Amy says.

She skates to Mo.

"Look at the bottom of your stick.

It's facing the net."

Mo moves his stick.

Now it's not facing the net.

Amy hits the puck to Mo.

It hits his stick and goes the

other way.

"Let's go!"

Coach Mimi calls to her team.

"Practice skating.

Practice hitting the puck."

Amy hits the puck to Mo.

He turns his stick just right.

The puck slides toward the goal.

Mo practices skating.

He skates across the ice.

He skates by Coach

Mimi and looks down.

CRASH!

Coach Mimi shakes

her head.

Coach Mimi calls Mo's
team together.
They are the Ducks.
"You will all get to play,
but only six at a time."

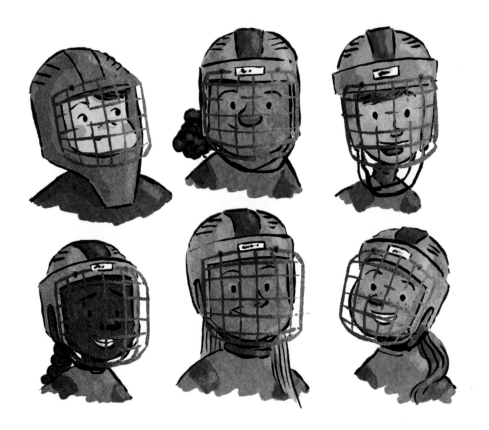

She tells the team who will start

the game.

"Max at goal.

Eve, Ben, Kate, Jane, and

of course Amy."

Amy is the best player on the team.

TWEET!

The game starts.

Amy is on the ice.

Mo is on the bench.

The puck slides quickly

across the ice.

It goes from the Ducks to the

other team, the Geese.

It goes from one player to another.

Amy passes the puck to Ben.

He swings his stick and hits

the puck, but he doesn't score.

TWEET!

It's the end of the first period.

"Let me play,"

Mo says to Coach Mimi.

"Amy will pass to me and I'll score."

Coach Mimi tells Mo,

"Everyone will play."

For the second period, she
takes Ben out of the game
and puts in Fran.

She takes out Kate and puts
in Alan.

Mo is still on the bench.

The puck goes from the Ducks to

the Geese.

The teams don't score.

TWEET!

It's the end of the second period.

For the third period, Coach Mimi takes Alan out of the game and puts in Jay.

She takes out Jane and puts in Gary.

She doesn't take out Amy.

The game is almost over.

The coach takes out Eve

and puts in Mo.

She tells him,

"Don't look at your feet.

Don't fall."

Mo skates toward the net.

He does not look down.

The puck slides quickly across
the ice.

It goes from one player to another.

Mo stands off to the
side of the net.
Now Amy has the puck.
Three Geese are between
her and the net.

Mo stands alone.

The bottom of his stick is facing

the net.

Amy hits the puck.

Whoosh!

It hits Mo's stick and bounces off.

It slides into the net.

GOAL!

TWEET!

The game is over.

"MO! MO!" the Ducks
and Coach Mimi shout.
"You won the game!"

"Mo," his dad says.

"You did it."

"No, Amy did it," Mo says.

"She hit the puck just right."

"We did it together," Amy says,

"and we won."